TO DREAM WITHIN A DREAM

A CEASELESS SOLILOQUY

TRIASHA MONDAL

Copyright © Triasha Mondal
All Rights Reserved.

"Why one writes is a question I can answer easily. I believe, one writes because one has to create a world where one can live. The world of my parents, the world of war, and the world of politics. I couldn't live in any of the worlds offered to me. I had to create a world of my own like an atmosphere—a climate; where I could breathe and recreate myself when destroyed by living."

-ANAIS NIN.

Contents

Acknowledgements

My father for being my most exacting critic. For being so forbearing as to listen, and give my verses an understanding. For telling me that one can never know enough.

Maa, for wearing magic in your eyes; every time I held the relic of a poem. In the dusk of despair, for making my heart sweet with hope.

Trinanjana, Rajnandini, Romit for having enwrought nothing but hope, faith, kindness and love.

Ayanisha, Sanyukta, Proiti for being the kind of readers, writers write for.

My grandparents, to whom I dedicate this book, in the hope of many more salubrious years of life.

• viii •

Thank you.

1. ME TO MYSELF: A SOLILOQUY

Under the splashing roof I lie,

while my heart and I, have an open conversation about how many tears does a man have to shed, before we consent him to cry?

how many lonely roads must the black kid advance for us to not slaughter him to die?

the country that shrunk into the poet's mailbox; she who holds the lofty mountains by her arms, and neglect in her heart,

politicians claiming how they don't 'take-things-for-granted' let them rescue the country for a start.

how long will the pianist have to kill the piano keys,

before he plays the ballad of peace?

how many depths must the grieving mother drown,

for there's a life beyond the river where the dead walk, she hopes to find her butchered son in such a lost town.

how many miles does the lost traveler walk,

for the milepost to guide him home..

he who is considered weak for ages- gassed, guillotined, poisoned and more;

whose mother awaits his arrival for centuries, by the burning door.

how many years for the history books to print how the country's wrinkled youth could no longer withhold the Kohinoor, the pride, her limbs which they divide
into forlorn regions whose names she doesn't get to decide.
the savage cruelty of the nation who allied, to plunder and loot
from about a time when people's rights were denied.
how many heights must the capitalists soar,
before there's nothing left to conquer
and when he attempts to sympathize with the poor, comforting him to not quit, when to his trusted god, that is the only thing he swore.
how many eyes must the government possess,
before they can watch the nation die,
to promise them a story where not bombs but bedimmed stars fell from the sky.
A stinging wind blew across my aching eyes, for to live makes one solitary
and as I hold the relic of my dying town's immortality
I howl,
how long until humans, to no longer lament the fate of humanity?

2. THE FINAL GAMBLE

In the deserted city of Syracuse

East coast of ancient Greece,

The guerrilla truce, the Jews lose

The monarch fell, the rules cease.

A vision of desolation, a deflating population, none remained

but young Artemis.

At dawn she sings a dismal song

Which goes like this,

Ave Maria, in armis tuis

Lucem inveniam

After her song, she trudged along

Between the woods, beneath the trees.

Artemis; mother to four- Lily,

Jose, Poppy and Theodore

After the guillotine attack, nearly died of young Jack.

Homeward, she comes only to stand before the helpless sight;

Of little Theo rummage for his sisters' lives

In the carnage, where the weak

were slain with the guilty man's knives.

Du soleil éclatant qui

Était autrefois leurs sourire

(of the bright sunshine; that was once their smiles)

Mid-slumber, her mind seized with thoughts..

('we are dead; we were alive; months ago; years back; we lived and laughed; we dined, we pined; we saw the pink and violet sky; tramp and trudge; then vision smudged; solitary we walk; but oh life; this life; this moment of June; this very minute; sleep; seize; how do they sleep; I sob, I sob.')

..what wild potion puts men to rest, even at the doom of their greatest unrest;

Then gently and silently, Theo caressed.

An echo of better days, when Artemis welcomed an unexpected guest,

The Grecian king stood before the charming miss,

Infrequent sighs; time invites her to shred her worth in front of his eyes

But now, Artemis gives out a loud and galled cry

"you see the fire under my rugged camisole, but not my people burning? Speak. For you never speak. Horsemen; pass by. Oil and tar; southwest wind; what do you think? Of war, this strife. Inexplicable splendor of the wind, speak? Of the wires they send? Nowhere a soul to call one's friend; perhaps you never think- of me, the people, ruins, Theo, rugs, bread, dying, dead. I shall walk out as I am, hair awry; undraped and walk the street to go cry with the gulls."

Colossus crumbling behind her; she sat upon the shore

smiling "my people humble, my people who expect nothing"
shanti. shanti. shanti.

[After Eliot]

3. SCHOOL OF THE DEAD (a passing thought)

Alas for the ravaged girl, pallid and time-torn;
Bewitched by some brutish beast; how long should she mourn?
In some nocturnal blackness; enwrought some
careless dream
Unbeknownst; whose weight has discounted smile from her mien.
Poor creature! a bedraggled fool,
Bled for louts, now feasting on you-
Why now lament your own child's theft,
For them to tell you, your childhood years' still left.
Soon, the deserts grew more deserted, no traveler left,
The brooks' thawed, birds silenced, all hopes bereft—
You bended to your God, hoping for some hope;
Pity such piety; where impotence is the heroic trope.
Why then, you embroider rugs around the wounds
Only to allow them to kill you again?
I reckon, the reason must be painful to explain.
How do you pardon those who
Bit your pretty heart in two

How old were you, when you buried you,
How old were you, when you bid joy adieu?
Halt the marching time; there's something I hear,
in this lone hour of despair
Or is it tender you,
still awaiting them to judge fair?

4. AN ODE TO MY HANDS

The outlines of my hands quiver in the rush of air, a whiff of decayed Syria hangs high;

it's wants unappeased, it's needs unattended- while we march with fresh and barbed instruments of torture.

Immense was such a night of suffering, where I ventured towards the dark of the shoreless ocean to tidy my hands. My hands have been the worst sufferers of an arsonist's mistakes-

The night of our attack, it lifted the butchered body of its own brother; who promised to return unscathed. Perhaps, war makes one a liar.

I feel strange pity for these timorous hands which fail to accommodate the wildest sobs, in lone and lengthened nights of grief; as though it is the one entrusted to ease my pain and put me to sleep.

And when I am in robust health, it adorns garlands around my hair, of white tinsels, purple and blue and I walk through fens and farmland into the unnamed civilization where men name me their God.

My hands drunk with fatigue, then crumble into clumsy fragments from nursing too much of my sorrow. A vile, incurable sore yet with such high zest it proceeds to undo the thickened ropes from around the neck of the mothers-

perhaps fastened to silence their misery. now they are silent.
these hands help me compose this poetry; an ode to itself. A
mere atonement for all the times I have made it bleed for me.
So, I write,
pardon
pardon
hoping it would forgive me.

5. FIVE SAD ENCOUNTERS, UNTIL I FOUND JOY.

It's five in the evening, as I sit by the cafeteria, sipping sorrows more than the latte perfectly brewed to give me a taste of modern royalty.

I tried writing missing reports in the name of poetry, for my grandfather who sleeps in his bed comfortably as if he had never been awake. He hasn't been awake.

I have no room for Maa's palak paneer thus follows a noisy altercation- how do I tell her I've tried nibbling my skin, every last morsel that has consummated my appetite; every time they told me they loathed my presence. A blemished blonde, a disgusting mess!

I wonder why, I smell of a mausoleum, when I have bathed again and again in the hot tub full of feral sobs, for little children to sail paper boats on, intimated with vague wishes of wishes coming true.

but then there was an epic massacre of history. As though an imprisonment in a democracy, an unlettered scholar-a proficient polyglot, the eternal penury of a capitalist. Hearts erupted in an ultraviolet chaos, slaughtered voices echoed, magnifying my arrival. I had found the ever-evading joy in the heart of grief. tell the society they have been inevitably luckless in glorifying the monotony of existing, of just being. For I am a process. I'm an element of yesterday, soon to be something greater than tomorrow. Knowing the unbeknown; of who I'm going to be tomorrow forever excites me to an unfamiliar degree. Perchance, a muse, a fatuous fool, a friend, a fiend, a child?

Oh to exist, is the sweetest and the bravest thing I've ever done.

6. PORTRAIT OF A MOTHER ON FIRE

Mother, you often baffle me
There's a world opening with your eyes,
A world of promising lies and unheard cries
Your limbs unfold like a newborn with each word you utter,
but you detest poems of joy,
as you detest anything that makes you stutter.
History unfurls as you take the world in your arms
your arms; bruised and almost broken
as you do the dishes until your skin withers with it.
for Maa, I see you shrinking like a burnt city
veins smashing like the shattered ruins of humanity.
Collapsed like a game of cards, what took a lifetime to built
Succumbed to sinned weapons, instantaneously it wilt.
Rue the day Maa, history is changing dimensions,
I bet they won't talk about your wounded skin and fragmented fibers.
They'll ooze the soul out of your tired lungs; you'll gag and choke on the inevitable cruelty—the cruelest collapse of mankind.
But I'll howl and wail and weep
To tell your story of how you hoped, even when hope stranded you.

You lived death, or did it live you?

I wonder why your God, taught you to love everybody but yourself;

As they feast on the blood, you bleed for them

Oh! Will your motherly misery ever end?

Yet do I marvel,

How you're the brutality of a soldier's sweat on the battlefield,

the beauty of the freshly cut grass after a year-long revolution.

Wiping the wounds off mankind's heart,

you called the world a museum of art.

And here I try to tell the story of your survival to the crowd,

of you, who pawned your dreams, only to live the dream of being a mother.

Thus, I write a homage to the home that you are; just as helpless, just as empty;

still hoping that the world would return your love.

7. DARTING INTO NOWHERE LAND

Day-long a duet of shade and light, amid the woods where I rent myself a shelter or a cabin; imagine, how lovely it would be if Indians talked instead of condemning. Existing instead of complaining it's futility.

how informing would it be, to exchange ideas instead of images.

To argue with propositions not popularity, life not looks.

And so together talking through Sunday's rising mist, to unpack one's walking shoes, to walk barefoot into the civilization they have burnt.

Don't carry the cell where statistics define your worth. neither a dictionary, for you are about to learn higher.

Carry jigsaw if you are shrewd enough, for hints are resurrected ruins shattered thither your path.

Pick up the remains, crammed into a little clay pot of how you drown a dead; you might find your life in it instead.

Don't take the cookbook, it's a feast. except you will be feasted on, for the fascists aren't the only true anarchists; look ahead, to the one holding poverty like a gun to your head.

They said, walk a thousand miles until your vision is smudged with fear. for only then, would you see the ruler's intent wide and clear.

And through the lonely wet road waylays simple girls, church-going. turn to them not with leering eyes but tenderness, to walk them to the altar to avenge for your unholy altering.

The period of illicit gloom will be over now, the grass springs for your grazing, preys wander for your hunting, doom frontlines in your territory;

but you have quelled it all, to find yourself amid the obscure mist, far from the perilous air; where our brothers are betrayed,

where a mother's life is made more bleak, every week.

And in the end, what is it, that is left? that is only what you need to live simply.

8. NOT RICH, BUT HUMAN

The other day, I complained about not possessing half of the riches my companions own,
mother inquired, whether a little family on the streets I had known..
and asked me to observe them for twenty days,
classified apathetic, if not in my conscience heavy it weighs.
There lived a woman across the street,
her deprived daughter crying herself to sleep.
Mother carrying baggages of deceased husband's bills..
while the little girl was eliminated from all her teenage thrills.
breathing grief and drinking despair,
her bread is agony, shredded rugs they wear.
shattered dreams under the master's feet,
when they beg for food, how inhospitably we greet.
They keep on dying again and again—once, twice they aren't aware,
but for a penniless sufferer do we sincerely care?
Care for the impoverished, the destitute, the deprived.
Show.
Show your concern, your modesty, your respect.
don't forsake knowing they aren't perfect but wrecked.
Tell them it's sanctioned to lose, but not to lose out.

Apprise that they are protected and cherished,

until the dusk when they have been perished.

their chronicle is of a different mayhem,

the sky rains oceans of tears, the flowers in the garden of their

dreams died many a times.

where the orchestra of giggles and uninhibited delight,

would not retire into thin daylight.

their world might not be embellished with fancy costumes

and vigorous party volumes.

they don't escort June nights with champagne or highflyer

wailing for more.

instead they can't combat the distress anymore.

its-pouring-with-rain

its-roaring-with-pain

rise-in-your-fate

fight-in-your-race

their slaughtered mouths trying to disclose the deception but

we aren't aware,

for the truth is overly heavy for us to bear.

Thus, let us soak their sob gently,

eradicating our underbred pride

in the vicinity of tenderness when we can stride.

Strength to their collapsed veins, withdrawing from the dark

and forlorn.

and tell them even though we are lonely,

we are never alone.

9. SONNET I: MUST I SING JOY'S SWANSONG?

How dost thou smile, amid thy well writ doom
han't misfortune thrust upon thee?
veiled under nature's silent, shapeless gloom
rested upon this trifling fantasy of eternal glee.

'Tis a thing impossible for my wild society
when fallen fairies visit men o'er sleep,
it costs a saint his piety, such an impropriety
so dear has't ye loved joys, thou now must weep.

What sayest thou prudent men
in lone and lengthened hours of grief?
hath thou mourned thy utmost then
or fie upon life, having believed in this disbelief!

And so I writ till my ink be dry,
and to live ever, to see nay man sigh.
[After Keats]

10. ALPHABETS

Inspired by Inger Christensen.

The beauty and the brutality coexist
midsummers and early falls exist/grasses, meadows and parks exist/disintegrating weak, weary of unending weeks exist/ gypsies asking for an address exists/dreary dreamers and optimists exist/sinking ships and blood inundated kitchen sink exists/trips to a burnt house exists/breakdowns and trip overs near the crumbling door exists/waves breaking on the desolate shore and the schoolgirl who waves at the world exists/flowers that wither and fall, to make glorious falls exists/ guns exist, chemical lit-up ghetto guns in archaic built and sufficient precision exists/gunshots and wailing women, terror and tremor exists/the scene of crime- bathed in a godforsaken drowsy light exists/the poisonous crumbling chlorine and cyanide exists/disparity and discrimination exists/class struggle and anarchy exists/aftertaste and afterglow exists/ oaks, elms, junipers, sycamore;, loneliness exists/lovers and dreamers exist/fragmented pieces of fleeting peace exists/ cannonballs and white dove exists/unholy alterings in front of the holy altar exists/wrinkled youth and merry declining years exist/wrecking balls and teens bawling riversexist/fiction exists/details and memory exists/fragile memory carving

immaculate memories exists/single words, the only sound, offerings exist/life and the lifeless exists/silent screams and loud emptiness exists/ imperfections of perfection exists/ insignificance in significance exists/the complexity of nothingness exists/the greed amid need exists/the magic amid tragic exists/passionate differences and vigorous contradictions exist/dying and undying exists/uncertainty of certainty exists/art and destruction exists/and the future, the future...

11. REVERIES ON FRIENDSHIP

As your friend, I vowed that I'll shout all the praises and admiration to push you to the path of repute,

breaking chains of mayhem and persistent dispute.

as your friend, I swore to fight the demons and right the wrongs,

to make them reckon that you can walk through a thousand hells—crippling and wounding, yet you stand strong.

I promised to mend your heart every time someone breaks it

uttering the most ludicrous joke to bring back your grin,

when despair aches you to the bone and perils to rip off your skin.

you were the home of the homeless, mother to the motherless; you renew life to the deceased. You were divinity who preached Bible is more than just a narrative, kindness is not just an investment, that the prayers were more than just a metaphor and the world is more tender than the present-day definition of tenderness.

But eventually, the promises died a slow death.

Annihilating in one's own handcrafted casket. Vintage photo frames captured our consummate smiles but were bereft of it in reality.

My memory doesn't hold the orchestra of giggles nor the smell of tender affection. Exhilaration now is just a farce, whilst torment seems to be more sincere.

You orchestrated to depart, upon which Dali would write a surrealist verse? like how Salinger had isolated Claire from his comrades and associates..

utterly unaware of how her valor, he eliminates.

Now I reckon why Van Gogh swallowed yellow paint, maybe he was fatigued being labeled as sick, being left out- as they considered him to be a forlorn inconsolable prick.

Plath embellished her poetry with affliction and agony, while Ted Hughes practiced his patriarch and infidelity.

So now, I won't walk into another coterie as I have stopped looking for soulmates to reassure grief is short-lived, but in a bar-parlor reading aloud my tormented poetry ricocheting between gunshots and guillotines.

And as Van Gogh said his final words, "This sadness will last forever."

12. A PRAYER FOR BECOMING

I have loved the idea of becoming what I want to be
dreams and reveries assuring it would find me.
the cries of anguish will eventually be long gone,
a path of paradise it will leave for me to tread on.
I dreamt of an ideal world, where bullied men and broken teens would ascend up again;
valiantly asserting their esteem- they'll regain.
gunshots and guillotines would ultimately be replaced with amiable hugs and negotiation signs.
a consummate world, free from present-day crimes.
I wanted to know why life wasn't on my side,
by and by reckoning misery is not an exciting ride.
where mankind would cease the race they run,
and stop carrying contempt behind their gun.
the apprenticed slaves would finally be liberated free,
and my desolate self would find the most contented me.
the girl who was abused and society threatened to slaughter her mouth,
would be benevolent enough to protest she's bold enough just like any other scout.
when the damp night and the piercing gale would not threaten to rip me apart,

when I would unravel why certain friends orchestrated to depart.

like how Marie Curie's radiation theory lied, and sorrow corroded my soul, like no acid before.

Keats writing poetry for his unrequited love,

was even more complicated than the velocity-friction curve.

how Plath's confessions were no deception,

and how Van Gogh swallowed yellow paint,

just to paint the world with a different perception.

Tonight I'll pray for us to thee,

for I wish to barter torment with glee.

Convince us that there is more for us to do,

and guide us through the strenuous path, assuring you will guide through.

hereby, we pray for salvation and deliverance from harm and sin,

and courage to embrace the distress with a comparative wider grin.

13. MIDNIGHT MONOLOGUE

Ah, beloved!
You smell of carnations of overwork.
I bought pearls for the neck you strangle to bed,
every night.
Smear kohl wears off from mourning cruel fate
I am enamored; with the hypnotic glow of those
tired eyes.
You put lotion on your chapped lips; but they wither
from the excessive lies you have overeaten for Thanksgiving.
Tonight, you must seal the wounds and call it art.
Why is that you speak to me of possibilities,
While chiseling hope out, of the first page of
your crimped daybook?
You dream of planting lilacs in your backyard-
while your limbs wilt, every morsel of you,
wither in the godforsaken neglect of the present.
Tonight, I invite you to my ruinous space-a bleak
land where little children build civilizations out of
quicksand.
Bring to me, the cracked plate, with grease on your
fingernails; from no appreciation of how
tonight's dinner, was just the delight.

For all this while, you have dreamt of writing words
tender like a holy cathedral; when you wake up
with folklores curled around the edges of your bloodstream.

14. ON MEETING TRANQUILITY

This is the luminous abode where I needed to astray, when I wanted to stay anonymous. but then again touched the shimmering quill grey waters synchronizing with the inadvertent arrival of the mist and soothed myself. I escaped to the oceans to catch breath during times of immense misfortune and daily drudgery.

Complain it to be unusual but the ship seemed to be navigating into nowhere, speculating on the sheer nothingness. maybe because I longed to decipher the immense obsidian. The side of the ship anchoring in captivity which is not visible to the world at large. Dark days taught me to laugh on the less melancholic days. But it seemed to me that the ship was in her battle of survival in its plight—tranquil but not fragile. she can encompass the worst of the summer storms. Her chaos was harmonized getting control over the dark clouds, ocean's vastness, blood of dawn but plunging on steadily pacing the gale upon her back.

Perhaps, it taught me to wander placidly amid the chaos and composure. to paint the dull and ignorant as they too; have a life. the ship seemed to me, an epitome of strength, courage, and flawless fearlessness.

Escape? I cannot because I'm vulnerable learning to strive valiantly.

Trapped? All those who mistake vulnerability for weakness.

Photographed by Romit Mondal.

15. HOW TO LIVE IN A WORLD THAT MISGUIDES THY FAITH?

I feel a grief so foreign,

I fail to locate its source.

Asphyxiated my organs,

Excruciating this pain,

A deluge of moving carcass that I see?

Or a bunch of grieving men.

I wail out to the Gods

And rummage through every sacred book,

by the idea of perpetual grief, is he just as shook?

Pray tell; I long to reckon,

where does glee flit?

of wilted flowers and mourning souls

is that land built?

Somedays, it arrives with distinct shades,

Of a poor man crying out to shelter his wife,

Or an innocent slain with a guilty man's knife.

The sun doesn't rise, the lilacs refuse to bloom

Perchance we live in a realm,

Indemnifying a thousand corpses' gloom.
So, I pray for us to thee
For torment to leave our body and freight elsewhere
an unfamiliar wound that hurts doubly so,
of a contempt mankind carries, the reason they never know.

16. REMEMBERING MY HOMELAND

I darted away to the streets of my damned homeland;

my homeland speaks a thousand languages but is tongue-tied.

My homeland shelters grieving mothers but is a refugee.

My homeland is a requiem of revolutions but is unarmed.

My homeland beholds the full moon on a summer sky, even after

the guillotine hit her eye.

My homeland stands tall for mothers but is a crippled limp.

My homeland paints with vibrant colors but is colorblind.

My homeland clings to religion but has lost her faith.

My homeland is a home of democracy but is eternally enslaved.

My homeland wears flowers in her hair when she stands in an arson.

My homeland dies in draught but weeps to rescue the rye.

My homeland screams into wilderness, but her people deafened.

17. LOST & FOUND

I stand amid a vigorous whirlwind of fiction and facts, of remembrance and ignorance.

I drown in the midst of a thronging crowd that takes no notice of me.

the next moment the crowd seems to tell me what to do.

As I reach the zenith of this nothingness, I forget what it's like to feel- torment, tenderness; anything at all.

I scavenge helplessly for the truth, which dines a costly dinner with lies. Lies that govern my truth.

This is indeed a ruinous space; the vacuum between me and what I ought to be.

and in such a vigorous contradiction I slow-dance with my incapabilities.

Every morsel of which has more to learn, to unlearn. a visionless vision, a faithless faith.

I disappear in this wake; for it is my deeper dream. and so does my identity. all of it; fleeting this minute-

my knowing, unknowing, senses, and passions.

"Who is it, that I am?" "Who is it that I'm becoming?" an element of yesterday, soon to be something greater than tomorrow.

18. MUSINGS & CONTEMPLATIONS

- Don't complain that I have grown up when to your reassurances I would no longer smile, my radicalism wouldn't be too mild. But I'll howl and defy why's that you suppose "the world works this way," hoping to avail a self-help manual to keep torment at bay. Don't lament if I'm no longer subtle as I used to be. When you used your best opportunity to slaughter the child in me.

- Forgive me, for I cannot verse poetry about mirthful smiles and promising lies. I have been damned right from the start—a refugee in my own land before I could call it home. Befitting solitude next to love; I who was robbed of joy, before I learned how to smile; must be exempted from the need to write at least one sweet song of delight—when in the discourse of fate, misery has been my much loyal companion.

- For most days, I am rather a corpse, sitting on my solemn grave, watching my mourning funeral—embellished with obscure nights and unlit skies. My mind; an anarchy. A tenant under a master's behest—paying rent for my existence. My voice goes unheard, somewhere amid the lost smiles in the inglorious crowd. But O Master, avenge my eyes, for it dreams within a dream; some of which shall keep me alive forever.

- I wrote five lines of poetry and a song of despair. Five skies I have gazed at, yet five-thousand to gaze in my awakening; my deeper dream. But until my wake, I long to write more of all the things I fail to say..know why I use ellipsis in place of full stops—in life, I must be too afraid to cease. Come! who might, make your grand arrival—for I'd drink from a cup not knowing which is sorrow, which is joy. And in time, it may constrict my throat, corrode my limbs, despise my penmanship. But I desperately need to make sense of the poetry that writes me, comforts me, consumes me. Feed on me, until my ribs show—bruised, decayed, shattered. Now all that remains is love.

- Her heart dwells where she can revive from her grave. A clandestine land where she builds her own God. Lured by the beauty and brutality of nature, bereft of it arises an inevitable ache, invoking the metaphor of death. Of the lifeless. She cannot bear to exist sans it; for the body annihilates from within and she cannot

remember what comes after that.

19. TO DREAM WITHIN A DREAM: THE TALE

That night, before going to bed, I asked Maa for the umpteenth time, about what is wrong with me, as Mrs. Brown says her kids are too sane, to talk to an eccentric like me. I wanted to make friends like every schooler of my age, but somehow an obscure mystery sat between us like a third person. Like every other time Maa reassured me that I am just as much normal, as all of them and have nothing to fret about. Running loving fingers through my hair she said, "My dearest Vanya, there's nothing wrong with not being able to fit in. You will, with the right people."

"But then how do I talk to them, eat lunch with, tell them all about my day?" said I. "Write letters to them. Let out everything you want them to know. Tell them in many words how you love them and how all of us are stained with a desire to be loved." Said Maa, with an unblinking gaze, repressing of what looked like a sob.

A stinging wind blew across my aching eyes as the alarm rang at 7 in the morning. The air was heavy with moisture, from all the tireless sweat of the busy bustling city beneath. Briskly getting up, I got dressed somehow gobbling up the toast all at once, packed the bag and left readying myself for the day. Dad hurried down the stairs to say, "Anytime it happens so, that you might start feeling unwell and need a little slumber, call me immediately." "Dad your concern baffles me as much as it contents me. Why would I want to sleep in the middle of the day?"

There! The school bell rings for the Literature class, and in the hallway, I heard an echo of a familiar voice, that I'm especially not fond of; but it seems like I'm inured to hardship lately. "Look at that dunce Vanya Flores, an imbecile who should consider therapy without further ado. So, tell us you, not even half as virile as one can expect you to be; what fable have you got for us today? I wonder, which aisle of children's books you scavenge, so as to have such an amusing wagon of ludicrous fairy tales."

"Enough Burke. Stop with all your sordid games. Your heart is barren by nature, alloyed with pitiful insignificance. Get away for you stifle my breath and constrict my throat. And I mention this in you and your disciples' hearing these aren't made up fables. These aren't fiction. It is the reality that stains my peace of mind, alloys my memory, contaminates my conscience. I failed Mr. Beaufort's French test the other day. My mother was too tolerant to say the test is due, just to ruth the remorse I felt already. But I know made her upset. It suffocates me with enough distress for you to have to cause some more."

"Well, this is why we think you to be loopy for the test is actually due today. Save up this rhetoric to trouble someone else through their day. No wonder why you make everyone nauseous." Said Burke giving his companions a nudge.

The bell for recess rang and I occupied a solitary seat in the cafeteria. The view was torturous however. Everybody was accompanied with their friends and for all I knew I struck their chords of antipathy but not Nate's. I remember he was a good friend until his friends coerced him, to give me a good wallop, to prove his might to them. Mustering courage I walked up to him,

"Hey Nate, don't you feel even a pang of remorse for what you did last week? Look at my forehead how you have wounded me cruelly. And to make things even worse you tried to scar Cecelia too. And now you deliberately shun us, to evade bearing an apology." Nate remained indulged in ecstatic contemplation, then said "You should consider not daydreaming in class. And who in Christ's name is Cecelia? if you would care to face the mirror, you'll see how you are entirely unscathed and something of that sort hasn't happened yet, but it will, if you further rile me with all your ridiculous fables."

I felt unhappy about accusing him but I very vividly remember it all happening. And how could he unknow Cecelia? That was the day I met her. When she hurried out of her classroom to protect me. Perhaps he was not tricking me. But everything feels like a blear deception. A meaningless hoax. I don't know what to believe in anymore. For all I know, it gnaws every morsel of my flesh within.

That was when I promptly remembered what Maa had said to me; something about writing letters to the ones, I dearly love. And the one who is imprinted on my memory is my sweet Cecelia- the only escape, to have breathed the breath of life. I proceed to write,

To Cecelia Jones,

10 Downing Street London,

SW1A 4 October

You have added to your sins by not coming to school without telephoning. You reckon how it is all here. I haven't seen you for over a week now. Not hearing from you, for long causes me distraught. For you see, you are the only soul that is my friend. They say they don't know who you are. Burke has been vengeful. Nate claims to not remember anything from our day of discord. The day he bruised my forehead. He says, I am deceived. I don't see a scar on my forehead though. I cannot keep pace with everything that's going on. They call me a freak. You were there, that day. You, who make my heart sweet with hope, why do you elude me now? I don't get what they say. All of this cannot be a mere dream. It's the reality that I see. Every night, I have trouble sleeping. Some days it comes to me silently. The other, it pulls me into its cold territory. Hijacks me, my entire being, until there's nothing left. How can they unsee our brothers getting betrayed and butchered? Where doom consummates one's appetite and a brewed teapot of sorrow quenches the thirst. When did the fate of humanity turn this unfortunate? They say they don't see these around. Perhaps, they don't want to. Or maybe I really am but a freak? Please don't elude me, sweet Cecelia, I cannot figure this out alone.

Yours affectionately,

Vanya Flores.

The next morning, the first thing I did was visit the Principal's office,

"Good morning Mrs. Queller, Cecelia Jones of the other class has been missing out on schoolwork. I wish to take a few days' leave to go check on her if you permit." "Vanya, I appreciate your concern, but you must have been mistaken. There's no Cecelia registered under this school."

"Headmistress you ought to be making fun of me as the boys do. How can you not know the one true friend that I have? Who doesn't trample me or my efforts? The only one that cares?" I broke into tears; I tried phoning her a thousand times but I didn't know her number.

I wrote her letters but instead of stamp, I put hope.

To Cecelia Jones,

71 Howard Street Southampton,

UK SO53

Dearest Cecelia,

I don't know where you are right now. I don't want to. I just want to thank you. Thank you enough, for being more than just real to me. For existing, however, you were. Thank you for you didn't bury me with an inferior mind. For making me realize I have done no such deed to deserve no friends. The period of elicit gloom is over now for you have made me fathom that what they talk about might even be true but that doesn't wound me, even a whit, knowing it doesn't make one any less different. Any less meek. Any less human. You have struck peace in my innermost. You have shown me how I have so many shades of the world to contemplate within my own heart. That might call upon sneers and contempt but doesn't mean I am not on the right course. But I might have been different. Akin to them as they wished. Perhaps like you? Not a commonplace sinner but someone whose faith equals God. However, I now know, how they will heartily agree to be friends with me. Love me, for who I am in the restless tides of time. I have faith, someday it'll reach your address. We'll meet in between the lapses of life and death. And if perchance, the nightmares were/were not a reality, thank the stars; you are the tail end of a sweet dream. And I hope to never wake up. I long to never recover.

Yours affectionately,

Vanya Flores.

Sussex.

XXX

www.ingramcontent.com/pod-product-compliance
Lightning Source LLC
Chambersburg PA
CBHW031245130726
47988CB00008B/3250